THE LOST ART OF STARING INTO FIRES
selected poems from the University of Winchester, 2010–2022

The Lost Art of Staring into Fires

selected poems from the University of Winchester

2010–2022

Valley Press

First published in 2022 by Valley Press
Woodend, The Crescent, Scarborough, YO11 2PW
www.valleypressuk.com

ISBN 978-1-912436-81-1
Cat. no. VP0198

Cover artwork by Katt Grover.
Cover design by Katt Grover and Peter Barnfather.
Text design by Peter Barnfather.
Edited by Glenn Fosbraey.

Printed and bound in Great Britain
by Clays Ltd, Elcograf S.p.A.

Contents

Foreword

Poetry is often referred to as a 'lost art' in The West. Readers are unsure of what they should look for in poems, whether they should be looking back or forward in time to find its necessity. The unpredictability of all that is going on can quickly convince one that verse is not the right thing, right now, to stare into and have that inner wisdom, or crystalised moment unlocked – maybe you're too busy in the dark, trying to find the right light?

The poets of University of Winchester write with a rejection of such a pretence. Now is the time for verse; now is the time for *their* verse. Within these pages you will witness lyrical wonder, personal excavations, sheer precision in form and romantic situation. These poets are bards, lyricists, confessionalists, satirists, irreverent surrealists – all writing with such a fire and heart that your hands may catch sparks as you read these pages.

The Lost Art of Staring into Fires is the inaugural poetry anthology of University of Winchester's alumni and current poets, published by Valley Press. Among its pages are prize-winners, such as the seminal Kaycee Hill and innovator Summer Young, as well as stalwart bards, namely Steven Mizen, who have changed the contemporary poetic landscape with their style, composition and control of language. There is a breadth, confidence and innovation within this anthology that mirrors the very essence of poetry; that it takes many forms, and all of them are for you, the reader to seize. Witness the mastery of imagery from Beth Philips & Lawrence Nicholas; belly-laugh at the gallows humour and surgical wit of Jack Stacey and John Son; feel the emotions run with Clare Holman-Hobbs & Matt LT Smith. There are quirky bangers from Sophie Edwards and silencing moments from Gracie Marsh-Bawden. There is poetry for you here that changes what poetry is, as we know it.

This is an opportunity to thank the tireless support of the poetry teachers at University of Winchester; Julian Stannard, Mark Rutter and Kass Boucher, all who have stood for poetry's multiple forms and functions, as opposed to truncating what poetry should be according to tradition – you have begun and progressed so many voices in contemporary poetry. A further thank you to the unyielding and courageous Glenn Fosbraey, who has assembled these poets here, encouraged their submissions and kept the grammar in check – Lord knows we need this.

I have been warmed by reading these words again; reading the words of my contemporaries, my former students, all of these inspiring voices gathered here. Come, take a seat by the campfire – let their language stoke the flames in the darkness.

Antosh Wojcik

Cigarettes

Matt L. T. Smith

I grew up in a house built on lung cancer
family dinners picked from tobacco fields.
School clothes smelled like Nan and Grandad's house
even when I didn't visit.
Even after Grandad's triple heart bypass,
after sticky blood, after Nan drowned in reverse
and came back with dementia.
Black pudding and sticky toffee looked the same,
but only if I thought about it.
Pork doesn't look like pigs when I'm eating.

My clothes smelled like refinery chimneys,
like Nan's miracle tablets that turned oil into wine,
there's a faint smell of leather on my Mum's side.
My clothes smelled like sweat, like hard work,
like "This is my house, my wife, my kids,
and they all smell like cigarettes."
But Dad would never touch the stuff.
My brother would.

Dad told him lungs aren't a refinery,
tar will only gum up the machine
and he can't fix him,
Can't listen for the rattle in his cough,
ears trained to hear the sound of broken
it sounds a lot like silence.
Sundays were never quiet.
My brother rolled another cigarette,
told me: 'our clothes already stink of smoke'
He's just trying to cover up the smell.

I said 'I'll never touch the stuff.'
He said "You will."
I didn't.

Dad worked nights at the factory.
We kept quiet getting ready for school.
His grizzly snore let us know he wasn't broken
he was working.
At the factory, Dad would sit and listen
to the hum of the machines.
They sounded like Sunday roast.

Dad's redundancy sounded like silence
and smelled of cigarettes.

Lemon Squeezer

Matt L. T. Smith

After Nan passed away
we collected up all the things her dementia brain
tried to remind us.
Motorbikes in black and white,
my five year old face taking a bite
into her golden wedding anniversary cake
before it's even sliced,
teeth smooshing into the icing,
face screwing up at the realisation that it's not chocolate.
I asked Nan and Grandad if I could be in the picture
when they cut the cake, with my stomach in my forehead.
When the family said cheese I remembered I was hungry.

In the museum of Nan and Grandad
were stacks of paper, bills, letters, proof of life.
In amongst the papers, mixed in with the gas and electric,
was a poem written by Nan's Grandad,
Mum's great Grandad,
my great, great, Grandad.
Rhymes written in the accent my Mother lost.
The accent that cooed from the corner of Nan's kitchen,
sat in her chair, in front of the cupboard stocked with Sugar Puffs,
with a cigarette hanging out of her mouth
as I pretended a lemon squeezer was a spaceship
in the absence of toys.

I realised, whilst reading great, great, Grandad's poem
that redundancy is the family curse.
He, like me, concerned himself with the men
who for years idle stood
with nothing for clothes and little for food.
The men whose kiddies physiques grew lower and lower,
as if gravity was conspiring against them,
after the shoe factory shut down in Cockermouth.
The factory where Nan used to work
before the conditions did her lungs in.

I wonder if she ever went back,
entered her Grandad's poem,
if the oxygen fled her brain
because it remembered that factory air
and tried to will it back into existence,
tried to be her Grandad's angel
who would save the brave people from hunger and cold.
Her tobacco lungs had already tried hard enough
to breathe my Dad's factory back into existence.
I wonder if great, great, Grandad
ever wondered if his great, great, Grandson
would be writing about the same thing
eighty-four years later,
over three-hundred miles south,
our stories only separated by time and distance.
Or maybe only Nan realised that time is that cyclical.

I should've pretended the lemon squeezer was a time machine
rendered myself four-dimensionally jet lagged,
given myself whiplash from looking back.
It's not like a writer's body clock could get any worse.
I wonder if great, great, Grandad was the same.
I wonder if he wrote his poem out of time, like I would.
All it would take is a lemon squeezer to ask him.

I wish I could've put Nan's memories in the lemon squeezer,
squashed everything sour out of them
given Mum a happy childhood to relive
on the days that Nan thought Mum was a kid again.
I wish I could put all our childhoods in the lemon squeezer
juice the silence out
get the machine humming again,
but I'm face planting a cake forever.
It always tastes of jam
never chocolate.

Currently Out of Order

Kane Holborn

The disabled toilet is disabled today,
yesterday
and tomorrow.
The disabled toilet is disabled.
The disabled toilet is disabled.
The disabled toilet is disabled.
Please feel free to use the disabled toilet
upstairs.

Fuck Platonic Love!

Kane Holborn

Epigraph from *My Left Foot* (1987) 'I've had nothing but
Platonic love all my life. Do you know what I say? Fuck Plato!
And fuck all love that's not a hundred percent commitment!'

Fuck my left side
that does not abide.
Fuck Platonic love!
Fuck Plato!
Fuck the fox that
makes me a Phoenix.
Fuck the plastic Rose
that makes me empty.
Fast-forward love that
explodes the plutonium.
Fuck my tryst
with the completionist.
Outlaw the platonic.
Don't outlaw
physical flaws.
Make all love
a hundred percent!
Deconstruct
the construct.
Fuck fifty percent equality.
We're equal: don't maximise
the axiom!
Who cracks
the axe?
Only the universe sighs
when a tree falls
in the forest.

Tastes From Budapest 1993

Kane Holborn

Did you happen to visit Budapest in 1993?
Up and down the ladder chair.
Conductive education
in musical repetition.
Colours, smells and tastes served as
memories instead and
you only recognise poverty retrospectively.
Labda! Labda! Labda!
A warm bowl of Goulash Soup.
A part of the local language slips in…
Travelling everywhere by villamos trams.
You don't remember poverty
when you're only two years old.
Only pungent warm orange juice.

Eating Trends

Antosh Wojcik

Goldfish live like starlings in Warsaw –
everyone's short-term memories
gulped out of their heads by spongey clouds.

They pang the heart and a sense of time
that is no longer ours. You can get freeze dried
bugs like grazing nuts now –

there's that coffee joint that sells lavender hot choc
and bowls of jasmined locusts. We deserve it.
Under-resourced Satanists still buy Coca Cola.

Satan made me sweat after I drank the sleep
out of the B'N'B waterbed. Babcia didn't know
hounds had souls till she looked into the eyes

of a dead Weimaraner and remembered
it had chosen never to hunt anything,
not even her kind.

Time moves on, eating itself.
We hang on the air as the remains of its habit.
My currency is four of itself here.

That's two weeks not worrying about the electric.
The storm's not letting up.
Pass the sauce would you.

Yard Sale

Antosh Wojcik

Yeah, yard sale's been going for years now.
Weird thing – the English neighbours
don't seize the chance of owning
a part of me so obviously.
Those Americans were right there,
practically taking the turf of the yard
from beneath my feet.
Lil' local landgrab over here.
Yard gangs hitting the neighbourhoods
for their lawns. I swear, whole yards gone,
the stately live in gardeners running
out yelling as if the stolen ground
approximates to those carpet bombed
places too far away to think about right now –
But if we were going to think about it.
Picture the scene. A yard sale
on napalmed ground still scarred.
Cheap pitches, believe me.
I mean, you own it if you bomb it, right?
Those kids running out of the distance
mostly mouth. My ex, arrived at the massacre fields
30 years later, six foot, kinda Aryan.
She was surprised that the local people
didn't like Westerners too much.
She flew there on pocket money.
Carboot sale rent-a-genocide.
Gone for six months and came back
with that milky far-offness in her eyes
that all suburbanites have, you know?

Anyway, Aunt Cathy's walking stick is $30
and I'll throw her ghost in for free,
special offer, it's all got to go.
Not much time left.

a lawn ache

Antosh Wojcik

the lawn aches
mum wants it replaced

with something that won't breathe
a crying man missing my sister

has come to install nu-grass
we dig up the previous animals

in preparation
bones in shoeboxes

fossilised pornography lives here too
hands pulling disembodied flanks

inwards in the stills – I bury my harms
and lusts in the lawn

porn, living like overgrown canines
in the lawn's mouth –

the lawn will be scalped for its suffering
maybe I'll come here at night

with my colonial DNA
knees down

I'll think about everyone shot
and accept responsibility

Some Paradoxes

Antosh Wojcik

for RL

We're all born into a river that we can't perceive,
its current unchanged by action, its banks unreachable.

At my most tired, I joked about dipping into other universes
and borrowing energy from other versions of me

so I could keep going through this universe.
I was mid-miracle and had to sustain.

You humoured the joke.
There are oceans within oceans and below them,

giant beings exist at the speed of thought,
gravity so scarce their bodies barely boundary

with the atmosphere they live. I have a hunch
that's where everyday miracles end up.

We had a lot of things in common with those in the sea.
Came the time you tested a paradox

in which your exes were at your house
and I was in the living room,

planting extinct ferns into the carpet.
It played out like a loving scenario;

I was bringing life to things that had passed.
Really, you were telling me I was now part of your past.

We, the exes, left the house together,
dudes navigating the same post-miracle world.

Couldn't exactly go for beers, either.
Decay is an exacting process of time.

We all get exhausted, then invent a future.
Luck is whether or not that future happens.

Still, there's a time that plays in the cinema of my head;
we are cycling through fields.

There are horses dreaming,
laying along the earth, their legs running on the bare air,

endless, a run within the run within,
their horse-friends looking over them.

You are laughing on your bike behind me,
resonance of a cello string bowed with horsehair,

the suspension of a wave without decay.
I keep my feet on the pedals, never stop, lucky.

Compass

Clare Holman-Hobbs

We are two sides of the same coin,
and joined by the gentle touch of our fingertips
from seas that stretch across acres of untouched land.

Above those roots I will walk, and take pilgrimage
past my reflection in your mirror,
wherever that is.

I will follow, your western star,
to the east, from my east and find you.
I will find you.

I look into the dark shadows,
past the door that stands
ajar.

The cracks of the landing light
stream through and comfort me
because I am, waiting.

Return, my lost love,
my twin,
the veins of my past.

They bind me to you, the blood I lose I find in you,
and like compass points, we join at the head,
even though our legs stand far, far apart.

You are my sole mate,
stitched on
or attached with soap.

Empty Apartment

Clare Holman-Hobbs

I feel, like none of this is real.
So untouchable, that I fear I may be left, to decay
in the confines of my empty apartment.

I drink gin with the curtains closed
and I contemplate you,
and existence, and our existence.

I sleep in the large hours
and sit awake,
pacing, in the small ones.

I take the lid off my pen and bleed,
trying to articulate what I mean when I say we're not humans.
Feelings.

Fingertips against soft skin, touching foreheads,
Eskimo kisses, and hair tucked behind ears.
The clock ticks like your heart beat against my spine,
   and I remember.

I sit and contemplate the emptiness,
yet I'm full of pine needles and belt buckles,
   and the way you undressed me with your eyes,
not with lust but curiosity, because I was just that girl
   from that town with that smile.

You saw me in that light. I remember it,
and how I don't understand myself, or this, or us,
and your arm around my shoulder as we walked
   back to my empty apartment,
dancing through the dark shadows.

I led and you followed.
And I knew that it was real from the start.

Kindred

Clare Holman-Hobbs

I walk up to the big house, where
you wait for me with your whistle
between your teeth, the sound of music
reminds me of watching another person
walk away.

Last time, it destroyed me.
It's still going to hurt either way.

You live here now, you told me.
Talking in whispers.
I know you, I know the way
my shadow dances on the wall
beside your bed. I cradled
you. I don't want to share
you.

There is a cherry blossom
between us, that
keeps me from seeing you.
How can you leave?
How can you leave when
I'm yours.

Appendix: we are victims
of time, of distance, of the lack of
context. Love letters written
without sound, we are patrons
on the empty side of the bed.

Leap Year

Clare Holman-Hobbs

after Ulysses

We would be twentytwo in November,
so I planned for the summer jumble sales,
while we were eating parma violet roses, and I was waiting.
You didn't like the eating part, and so
just like that you left, when
snow covered the ground on the 29th
when I was waiting, waiting, waiting
to ask you, and it would be like heaven.
Instead it felt like
hell had frozen over, with all of my heart.

big world

Danny Adams

people are being hurt by vibrations
mumbled from rooms they aren't even in

like children hearing other children
hearing their parents fight, thinking
there is something wrong here
but not with me – yet nonetheless
they are compelled to scream | point | point | cry
until their eyes bleed blood so unfamiliar
that it may as well be blue

this is the difference between criminal damage
   and crumbling in the wind
when the earth does not quake
   but bodies still part at the skin \ fold back
exposing insecurities – vulnerabilities like raw flesh grazed knees
from running fast and blind in icy playgrounds
where the monkey bars were too cold to touch
without leaving behind a little too much
taking with them a little too much rust
            reminding the rest of us
that there is far more oxygen in the world
   than most could imagine

far more to the world
than most will give it credit
   those karmic debt collectors scared to knock
   for fear of the very debtors that fear them

this is the difference between a peaceful protest
and the noise in their Molotov minds / years
of fidgeting thumbs / unrequited love / yearning
for cocktail ruptures – a primal need
for broken glass
    and burning buildings

the blood of the enemy is not enough

    there's a reason writers cringe
    at the thought of burning books

    a reason sculptors memorialise
    the then, the now and the what might be

this is the difference between mutually assured destruction
    and total tilted anarchy
when there are sides in all directions
but no one left alive to see them

most people handle violence
about as well as they handle their own failures
which is to say: they don't

not a child in this world has ever been good
at idle games of hide and seek
    their feet stick out at every opportunity
and giggles of joy and anticipation
have never been indicative
of where they were before
or where they might be now

this is the difference between playtime and history

    no one ever erased their childhood
    never rewrote the most important memories
    which made them what they are today

a tilt of the head and a long look in the mirror
is all it takes to step beyond the fragile veil
                      of self
                indulgence
          and into the future

hey man,

Danny Adams

I hope you are well
in these weird times?

apologies for my absence

atoms have a tendency to expand
are in the habit of becoming more dense
over time, like an arrogant self-indulgent dust.

sometimes looking into that space
is like looking for mushrooms
capable of un-asphalting themselves
through tarmac –   the distinct kind,
                    you know the one. like
                    the road on the grey side
                    of Southampton Central
             where the old Toys 'R Us used to be

                    I am sorry this email isn't an email
                    life is messier than hair accumulated
                    in the dead air of a virus-ridden stillness.
             there's a duplicity to that kind of growth, I suppose.
             an outwards force – soft – sometimes greasy
             but a force nonetheless.

        so comes an equal and opposite
whatever the hell that might be…

apparently, they never grow.
                atoms that is – and
possibly more relevant to
our human experience, the brain.
they only retreat into themselves
                fold in and in and in
                become denser and denser
                like some fleshy origami
containing all the poems we're yet to write
                and all the rest we've ever written
                collecting like a stubborn
                                self-indulgent dust
                                which, some days
                        and likely in our days to come
                                slowly settles with us
                so that we forget they are even there
                just a cluster of imperceptible words
perpetually taking up the exact same amount of space
forming the exact same ever-expanding space
between everything.

always connected but constantly disconnecting
like some dodgy Zoom call or Microsoft Teams

Dark-Haired Hilda
Replies to Patrick Kavanagh

Georgia Hilton

On Raglan Road I saw you first
a dishevelled man with heavy
black-framed glasses. So severe
you looked but you had a wound
that made you beautiful.

After we talked that first day, I
dreamt of you. You were walking
towards me very fast and purposeful
with an intent that might have been
mistaken for malice, had I

not loved you. I abandoned
caution at first. But my father gave me
a great gift when he said to me, Hilda,
you cannot eat words and air,
so I became a doctor
and married the engineer.

But not before I had given you
poems with your own name in them,
given you my youth. Let you open
the catch to a window in my mind,
thinking I would fly, but you had me
chained to a pedestal. I,

no marble idol, just a flesh
and blood woman. And you were always
an awful man for the drink, you said so
yourself, Patrick. Oh to think
I might have been one of those
sorry women who follow

their husbands to the pub screaming
for them to come home before they spend
the rest of the housekeeping. I might
be a creature made of clay, Patrick,
in fact, I'm sure I am,

but you have a brass neck
calling yourself an angel.

Salmon of Knowledge

Georgia Hilton

In the dingy attic
where we took those pills,
I had a moment
of perfect knowledge
as if I had eaten the Salmon
itself, and I knew then
that all my troubles
could have been averted
had I been American.

Had I been American,
I think it's no exaggeration
to say I would have been
more wholesome
and at the same time
more assertive – a certain
rough and tumble dynamism
being much admired
in the American girl.

I might even have played
Little League
with my baseball cap
turned fetchingly backwards.
Or been Best Friends
with an Alien Life Form.
I would have drunk
all the Pepsi Cola I wanted,
and my teeth
would still be brilliant.

How inconsiderate then
of my ancestors, not to have
emigrated, but instead
to have stuck it out,
miserably, through famine,
occupation, the chill hand
of the church. Now I am
almost an old woman,
with nothing left to me
but my daily habits –
my black tea, my hearth,
my porridge, television.

When We Were Young

Georgia Hilton

We ate the road,
devouring
miles and miles of it
like liquorice string
unspooling
into nights made liquid
by cats' eyes
and brake lights.

Never did I believe
the stars could be
outshone
until that one night,
when an eighty kilometre
sign outside Athlone
met us like the moon
at high tide – radiant,
impassive –

reflecting
not the sun's light
but our own headlamps,
making us
the agents of waking,
as we tumbled
urgent, thoughtless.

We must have startled
badgers in the ditches
when overnight we scratched
the spine of half
the country, how it
twitched and shuddered
beneath our wheels,
impatient.

The Lost Art of Staring into Fires

Georgia Hilton

When we were kids, we practised this:
the lost art of staring into fires.

There was no need to break the silence –
no one said, 'hey kid, what you up to?'

it was obvious we were staring into fires.
Watching coals collapsing into embers

is the only lesson in mortality I ever needed.

Elegy for my Tamagotchi

Katt Grover

the first time it happened I cried
just four days; an omen
from your motherland

I killed you long before I ventured into plants

when I forgot to take you to dad's house at the weekend
I returned to find your disembodied spirit
floating above a tiny grave

you died of sickness
you died of starvation
you died in a pile of digital excrement

sometimes you went alone
sometimes I observed
holding your hand or
holding a pillow over your face
depending on my mood

don't worry, I would whisper
you will be reborn again
and you were
which in hindsight
gave me unrealistic expectations
about death

Chicken Dream

Katt Grover

I had a dream about farm animals and the animals were talking to me. I couldn't understand them, but I knew they were talking, rather than just making animal noises. What are you trying to say? I asked them. A chicken came and sat with me. It was naked and so was I. I'm naked in about 90% of my dreams. What does this mean? Am I scared of commitment? Are all my teeth going to fall out? Do I secretly want to fuck my dad? I studied the pink flesh of the featherless chicken and realised its skin looked just like mine. Without its feathers the chicken could not fly. Without my clothes I could not go to work. I felt connected to that chicken. I laughed because it was funny that my nakedness made me 'too chicken' to go to work because nakedness is frowned upon in our society. I looked at my breasts. I looked at the chicken's breast. I blushed. The chicken seemed to be trying to tell me something. It spoke, what I can only presume was chicken at me. I still could not understand it. I stroked my finger gently on the chicken's naked skin. It did not feel the same as stroking a pre-packaged whole chicken from Tesco. My finger glided softly over it and it was warm. I didn't feel the need to immediately wash my hands in case of salmonella infection, although raw poultry is a particularly high risk. I felt bad calling her poultry. She wasn't poultry, she was a living chicken.

What is your name? I asked her. She did not respond in words. She looked at the sky then cocked her head so fast her neck broke with a crunch.

I woke up crying and confused and angry. I wanted to do something indecent. Like go to work naked.

As I nudely made my lunch, globs of mayonnaise found their way to my nipples and it felt wrong. Like that time I tried to mix sex and food; two great pleasures that should NOT be experienced together. I realised I could not go to work naked. I was frightened at the thought of paper-cut areola and those tiny paper moons from hole-punches nesting in my pubic hair. I threw the leftover roast chicken meant for my sandwich in the bin. I knew I would never knowingly eat it again. I didn't want to eat the animals. People would hate me because I was now a 'fussy eater'. I would have to fill in special dietary requirement request forms and my family would have to make separate sandwiches for me at get togethers.

Sometimes I remember

Katt Grover

the look on the bereavement counsellor's face
when she learned there would be no funeral
symbolic or otherwise

believe me when I say
I carried it around in my pocket because I thought it was
an ovary that slipped out

had truth been known I would not have
handed it to the doctor and asked if he could
pop it back in

that small translucent sac of flesh
that morsel of amniotic calamari pre-ringed and pork-pink
exactly what a singular deflated ovary might look like

throwing the foetal sac into my neighbour's wheelie bin was not
the troubled actions of a grieving mother
though the bereavement counsellor told her husband over dinner
that it was

so sad
they said
so sad

Mama Butterfly

Katt Grover

your biological mother was a cabbage white
she left you orphaned on my prized veg
must have heard of my no-harm organic methods of
humane and mostly useless pest-control

against the advice of my grandfather I didn't crush you
clutch of tiny eggs the colour of weak orange squash
I pinched your uterine leaf from my future side dish
placed you in a jam-jar and called my sister to tell her
I'd just become a single mother of forty

the internet forums dedicated to raising butterflies
warned me of your appetite
you were fussy and would not touch shop-bought brassicas but
long into the night you wailed for purple sprouting,
home-grown, a taste of home
the very same plant you were laid on and nothing else

my surrogate maternal instincts kicked in at 4am after hours
of lost sleep worrying you'd starve to death
what would the other mother's think of my undernourished
children?

I crept into my own vegetable patch and trawled up rows of broccoli
cut the stalks into little hearts so when you grew up
you'd remember I loved you

At the last bite you retreated into your moody chrysalides
eager to grow up, keen to leave home
when you emerged you were beautiful
we made an occasion of your maiden flight
fruit platters with sliced nectarines and pomegranates
you erupted into the air and I watched in horror as
blackbirds swooped down and picked you off in gulps

Contemporary Irus

Mike Redman Johnson

I introduce to you a man of pure
intent: so full of weighty generous
ideals that, heavyset and insecure
With shouldering their cold and treacherous
weight, is wont to topple floorward, as floor
receives him well as ocean Icarus.
And though it was not in him to be cruel
he was, at best, a mighty, marvellous tool.

To hotbed, cesspit of like-minded fools
he goes, drawn by the ageless pulling of
familiar desire, set in stool
by bar, to drown gilled sorrows, 'til the glove
of self is off in Dionysian fuel,
and muttering he shutters up his love
In opening the shutters of his jaws;
He surely was a walking awkward pause.

This clear delirium becomes the world,
all sensibility subordinate
to its distortions, until pain and cold
are dampened, and all other lights are cut.
The green apate light now seems to scold,
The warming gaze, no longer temperate,
and notes that once had airy brilliance
and joys are ringing now with dissonance.

See now betwixt the darkling air and he
come looming jagged monoliths of stone
from mother-night, recumbent on the sea,
that, kilned of reified betrayal's drone
are yet invisible, till finally
the leading ends: he finds himself alone
and wrecked upon them, realising now
he has returned to where he first was found.

Again the bar, again from off the rocks
he casts himself amid charybdis, and
into the liquid void, the opened box
that fills his mind with wrath and wraths command,
with visions of avenging fury, blocks
his breath and chokes his fist, but see: his hand
uncurls and holds itself, his anger cools
alone. It was not in him to be cruel.

But see now how that murk and murky fog
is cut by tones euphonious and warm
that, washing over him with lightest touch
of lighthouse beam, all clarity and calm,
'till hands are in his hands, and led along,
the tempest straits, he tastes with palm, a palm
of touching grace, and some new drunkenness
is on him, drunk anew on touch and kiss.

Do the Robot

Mike Redman Johnson

I'm a Sex-Machine running on Windows 97.
Due to frequent system errors I can't maintain an erection
but I will woo you with my preface catalogue of chat-up lines,
though my library's not been updated since 1999.
Download a PDF on surgery; I can even give you a face-lift,
but, really, there's no need.
It's like you're holding down shift
the way you give me Sticky Keys.
How about I set the mood?
I've got a candlelight app.
And for music, we'll use Youtube,
'cause my iTunes has crashed.
You needn't worry, my interface is User Friendly.
Keyless entry, cook you breakfast,
Continental, complementary!
No ego to vent: I've no need for penis envy.
If we get to mine and you're parched,
for a small charge you might take part
in a liquid repast from my mini-bar.
For a snack you might part
with a bit of cash to my vending machine;
I've got Snickers and Mars Bars.

I'm made from recycled Scalectrix
with a recycled Code of Ethics.
I service anyone from school kids to geriatrics.
And I accidentally swapped my g-spot coords for Tetris.
A quick search on Google'll tell me what I need to know
and it'll only take a few hours for the browser to load.
If that's a bit slow, don't worry, you won't be bored.
I can load up Space Invaders; see if you can beat my high score.
Now when we get down to get it on
I've a variety of settings to choose from.
From rotate to vibrate,
speed settings 1 to 21,
at 50p a rate
5 quid, you can't go wrong.
If you were my laptop
I'd turn you off,
'cause you are too hot.
Now let's track back
to my pad
so you can do the Robot.

Simple as That

Mike Redman Johnson

'It's as simple as that,' she said,
snapping her fingers and
sliding the drink to the side.
Sly and sinister, the upward sloping side
of her mouth shapes a smirk;
to her, I'm sure, a symptom of assured success
but to me, a snide snipe,
a subtlety that says to me
that stubborn sense of certainty
must be snubbed.
'Simplicity', I say, 'is a fallacy.'
A blanket woven of idiocy
and cast over complexity.
'But' she intervenes 'you're being obscene!'
'This is a simple matter, simplicity is key.'
'A key of sorts, maybe,' I retort,
'But this key fits the tumblers of a dummy lock.'
'What' she asks 'are you getting at?'

I've peaked her curiosity,
and honestly it's a shock to me
to have reeled her in so easily.
'I'll begin with a query.'
Try to be as literal and empirical
when you come to approach this,
form a theory, and try to reveal to me:
Who is the world's greatest environmentalist?
Before you answer, I'll warn you
it's not some tree-hugging fucking hippie,
it's not Ghandi, it's not Marek Mayer,
it's not EF-fucking-Schumacher,
and it's definitely not some Green Peace-esque,
fucking panda-hugging committee.
Her face set, statuesque and steely,
strained in concentration
and pruned from puckering.
Over the music

you can almost hear the cogs turning,
and as I sway, lay in wait,
she concedes, admits defeat
and poses no such theories.
'The answer?' she demands.
In response I dramatically gesture with both hands
and grin wide as I reply
'The answer is Genghis Khan.'
'Bullshit!' she cries!
'No shit!' says I,
As down is ground
and up is sky,
and on my life, I fortify,
I do swear to you I tell no lie!
'But to praise that mass-murdered
is surely a blunder.
His life was to corrupt and kill,
pillage and plunder.'

I step back in my mind's-eye,
realise that I'm being pretentious,
but I'm pissed and growing more so,
so onwards I venture.
And that, my dear, is exactly why.
Killing four million was his legacy and imprint,
and in doing so nulled their carbon footprint.
For every family that died
and village that fried
new trees grew tall,
absorbing Carbon Monoxide.
Clearing the skies.
We'd be in the shit
if it weren't for his nasty side.
'Okay,' she grins, 'well done, you win,
the line between black and white isn't so thin.'
Yay! I say.
'But,' she cuts 'this win means nothing.

Do you even remember
what we were discussing?'
Suddenly I'm lost.
I remember trying to be clever
and thinking I was succeeding.
I remember coming in from the wet weather.
I remember drinking.
I remember peeing.
Oh.
Then I remember vomiting.

I remember the shouting and the singing.
It's about this time the barmaid sighs
and beckons two bouncers to my side.
'It's time to go!' and before I know
I'm being thrown through the door,
Expelled outside to the gutter,
mud coating my clothes and hat.
'Why?' I cry to the bouncers back,
Looking over his side, he replies:
'You're barred mate.
It's as simple as that.'

the prosecutors

Mike Redman Johnson

a tribute to john cooper-clarke

the prosecutors prepare their persecution plotting preliminary
proceedings of a pugnacious disposition peeking and prying
repudiating privacies of the poor powerless pest a pre-pubescent
pup pimply and simple while the prosecutors plot the pest pops
his pimples unprepared palisading provisions paling in comparis-
on to the putrid repast pending his punishment but the principle
point points to the premature aspects of his disposition purely a
kid with problems typically pacifistic but pushed by depression a
prisoner of repression picked a pocket perchance a preference for
piff or possibly pints perhaps a pint past distortion passed his lips
that night some sap sipping paint-stripper multiple pint pots make
pisspot properly plastered pissed past the point of return not a pot
to piss in and progressing into the pronged police patrol though
disruptive indisputably a slip-up peak of punishment a slap on the
palm but the prosecutors have over plans persuasive whisperings to
the panel hand-picked jury of prudes and pay-offs past faux pas'
paint the portrait of a reprobate the pay-offs primed and pandered
to the prudes no problem to persuade the pest is pressed in a
prickly spot the prosecution is superior the pest is not paid in
perceiving the pest's pear-shaped droplet of overpowering penit-
ence imprisonment plunge and plummet a pickle the parents
didn't predict i present the po-faced prosecutors... pricks

Orbit

E.R. Hollands

Stardust.
That's what we are.
Cosmic anomalies cascading into each other,
  a cacophony of impossibility.

We are the by-product of the unlikelihood of the sun
  being in the right place
of the planets aligning
so here, today, I can sit with you on the sofa
as you play games in baggy shirts
and eat crisps.

The unknotting of the fate's tapestry brought you here,
to me,
in our little house on a roundabout street,
where the sound of the train
rumbles by like a comet
and the rent somehow always leaves before we're ready,
a shooting star of financial stability.

You lumber out of bed
tugging at the cords of sleep,
your limbs dragging themselves out of dreams.
My fingers caress your side of the mattress,
the crater that held you,
and I roll and smile and twist in the warmth,
a moon drawn to sun,
a satellite to its circuitry.

How many times have I launched
myself into the stratosphere
of someone
only for catastrophe?

Not by an explosion of fuel and shrapnel,
but by an emptiness
inside me?

A drifting, hollow, shrinking of me
Lost in the atmosphere
of we?

With you, this is impossibility.

Your were the first to
pull me in,
not swallow me

We coexist,
our identities not shadowed,
but brightened
by each other's company

Your gravity is not destructive
it is grounding.
Your presence is not domination,
it is harmony.

And what makes it all the better,
is that you have no idea,
that your orbit is more than love to me

It is home.

It is everything.

Boiling Point

E.R. Hollands

<table>
<tr><td>I don't know when it started.</td><td>Chck. Hiss. rrrrRRRR.</td></tr>
</table>

I don't know when it started.	Chck. Hiss. rrrrRRRR.
	Chck. Hiss. rrrrRRRR.
The shameful nudge when an inside joke pushed out in public.	
	Chck. Hiss. rrrrRRRR
Blue egg shell mornings; my toes ache from walking.	
	Chck. Hiss. rrrrRRRR.
Some nights it's cold war, in warm blankets.	
	Chck. Hiss. rrrrRRRR.
A gulf the size of the atlantic between us.	
	Chck. Hiss. rrrrRRRR.
And I'm left thinking if this is it.	
	Chck.
If this is how it all ends.	
	Hiss.
If it's better to forget.	
	rrrrRRRR.
Chck	the time on my phone.
Hiss	back is to me, sweat trickling,
rrrrRRR	roll over.
Chck	to see if I'm still here.
Hiss	breathing grates my ears.
rrrrRRR	remember I'm not his.
Chck	the beating of my heart.

Hiss
rrrrRRR

We both hear it.

Seize it quick, before it's gone,
Babe, he says.
I raise my hand.
It's okay

head is turning to me.
rhythm of our love.
Chck. Hiss. rrrrRRRR.

Chck. Hiss. rrrrRRRR.

I'll put the kettle on.

The Snow-Coloured Daisy

Hollie Davis

the snow-coloured daisy sways
gently in the summer breeze

dancing under the rosy light
of the setting sun

with the tall green
grass blades

to the rushing water of a nearby
river and the evening song of the
birds.

02/03/2021

Hollie Davis

Another day has passed, it's now the second of March. Yet I wake to the same grey rain, the same grey streets, the same grey houses, the same grey clouds that fill the sky like smoke, the same grey grass, dead and muddy like the leaves that rest upon it, the same grey trees that stand naked and empty like skeletons, the same grey routine, the same grey.

And the days morph into weeks, the weeks to months, they pass slowly, yet too fast for me to grasp.

But soon it's time for Spring to rise from her year-long slumber, sleepy and gentle, she'll run her fingertips along the ground and flowers like sunlight will bloom. She'll wrap the trees in a coat of green and kiss the sky blue. She'll take away the cold and ice and fill the days with song, and like everything does the grey will pass and colour will return.

To Be Unbuttoned

Gabrielle O'Connell

Bones, once spotless, are now pages darkening, shedding
nude brilliance. I am chapters and foliage,
twig-fingers demanding release from cupboard-keeping
and the steep curve of dusk-dusted silence.
A winged key to the invisible
and I am opening like a faucet,
becoming the shiver   puff   burst
of animal
the hot breath of the runner and the hunter
where ankle-to-ankle speaks of hoof and horn
limbs close to the ground, eating earth.

Deflowering Ophelia

Gabrielle O'Connell

I tucked a red rose into my hair
for my first time,
romantically adorned
like a Pre-Raphaelite heroine.
It didn't last long.

My frame drum
clattered in the bed beside us,
a cumbersome third.

I didn't bleed after, but I liked the pink
in my cheeks and the Chinese silk robes
made me feel like the woman
I'd supposedly just become.

For Her Son

Gabrielle O'Connell

It's there in the walls she builds,
boundaries enforced with veins of iron and teeth
that smite, burn, bite any hand planting violence
in her gentle son.

It's there when she cradles his secret tears,
quietly giving him back their language.
Every day she begins her work again;
the edges of her flame-tongue and quick fingers
turn sharper still as she picks words out of his heart
like threads from a mangled weave
undone by careless cruelties.

It's there in the stillness of her body,
conductor's hands unconsciously counting the beat
as the flow of his song breaks onto her cheeks;
words a sea against her hearing aids.

She stands too close, toes to the stage,
looking adoringly into his face.
The spotlight hitting her back
turns wispy orange hair into a halo of fire.
In the surging mass of drum and bass grinders
she's all alone, an island of love.

I fell in love with the builder

Gabrielle O'Connell

The gold of his ring clinked against the mug.
We discussed wall colours,
giving all the devotion we couldn't say
into laying the first coats of fresh paint.

When he left, I pressed shaking hands to seamed
cheeks, scalded pink, and swallowed the teenage
shriek rising out of a forgotten place.

Every day he was there I slipped
further into reality, the world
solidifying into intensity.

After forty years of marriage,
kind marriage, honest marriage,
build an annex kind of marriage –
I thought love already had a face,
a name.

My friend said, *at least you've known
a love like that.*
I couldn't bear her simplicity.
It wasn't a what if or could've-been passion.
I was alive in a way I never had been.
He constructed the world around me,
fitted me into a place that had always
been waiting.

I found the most important person in my life
and made him tea.

Evaporation

Gracie Marsh-Bawden

I am a river –
two homes
and everything in between.
I want to wrap my mouth around a beach
at each end.
I wonder if the salt tastes the same.
I wonder if the boats go down like
Fiz Whiz or Prozac.
I want my fingers to find their way into villages
– not flood nor puddle
but stream.
I want to run deep,
in a direction that is mine.
Maybe they'll name towns after me,
or maybe I'll evaporate before the year is out.

Heat Wave

Gracie Marsh-Bawden

A slice of life divides the room.
It cuts through a gap in the curtains.
You are asleep –

orange foam
twisted and squeezed,
it meets the walls of your ears.

I slide a stolen airline eye mask up and down
up and down my forehead
and wonder when the heat wave will end.

It is too hot to touch
and naked isn't anything any more.
Isn't a genesis or a bubble
or a gift.

Up and down and up and down.
Together we are deaf, numb and blind.

Except we aren't, really.
Together, I mean.

Marilyn

Gracie Marsh-Bawden

I always loved your waist
snatched tight as though pinned
behind your back
with a clothes peg.
How did you manage it?
Perhaps it was the under-wear
some torturous device
squeezing your centre.
A birthday clown twisting
a balloon,
so the air travels up
and spills over the top.
Perhaps it was the barbiturates,
though I can't claim to know much
about their effect on your waistline.

I never mastered that feline flick,
the neat line,
black against bright white,
bordering flirty eyes.
Though, I suppose
that you didn't either.
There was a team, I'm sure,
a busy swarm of professionals,
buffing and blending and brightening.
You were never alone
until the end.
Even then, they watched you
through the window
your last performance
on a very small screen.

The Roach Motel

Ian Goldberg

Checking In
Breakfast ends at 10am, officially. I enjoy tactile conversation and seventeen distinct gins on the drinks menu. The clientele wears unusually persuasive cologne. *It's a real brutalist throwback! I love the fact that there's no windows.* I chart each of my possessions as they're moved: the discarded coat, leather carrier, an espresso maker (tipped over, leaking fluid) and devise a system of notation.

The Abstract
1) If your organisation ceased to function what would be the wider-reaching implications? One notch to signify the intangible (what cannot be observed or proven) but these violations are felt intuitively and must be recorded. The toothpaste here is noticeably bitter and unyielding. Reminder: it's essential to keep all receipts as there may be entitlements for previously unstated benefits.

Wrong Floor
Coincidence mounts. The potted plant reoccurs and reminds us, in no uncertain terms, our legacy will be plastic and tasteless. The future remains a proprietary feature. A parrot makes veiled threats on the discovery channel. – *can't hurt you, we will hurt the ones you love.* The CCTV is only showing footage of empty rooms.

Odourless and Tasteless
Dissolute laughter through the drywall and the drinks go straight to your head, it's practically unbearable. Breakfast ends. I bloody my finger trying to find where the mirror and hardwood frame become mercifully indistinguishable. *Is that what I look like? Or is the glass just angled?* I can't sleep, it's like staring into the sun. The lights come back on. Revulsion is entirely non-compulsory.

R&R

00:00 blinks without pause. Last night, I dreamt of brittle men with bloated stomachs scurrying across the carpet. In the afterimage, I watch their mouths moving in time with their legs, clicking, sliding between distended sheets of wallpaper. Half-awake/half-dreaming: it's summertime, I'm throwing stones by the dry docks, Steve's RC helicopter spins out over the neighbour's backyard. A shadow passes under the doorframe. *If your organisation ceased to function.*

What would be the wider-reaching implications?

Statement of Confidentiality

There's no more room to carve under the desk. Any further dissemination of this transcript is strictly prohibited. If you have received this transmission in error, please… I'm running out of ways to adequately communicate how this feels. A colleague remarked. *Saddest thing, no one relies on you for anything, not really.* Strain, and you can hear it raining through the roof.

Checking Out
N/A.

Undergod

Ian Goldberg

Yes, there are dogs.
More specifically, there is
the underside of a dog   emerging pendulously.

It is mottled, and thinning
and unfamiliar in the way
most dog stomachs are.

"We are unaware of this side
of the dog," we exclaim, red-faced and
exhilarated when *Oreo* belly-flops
into the neighbor's pool.

Summertime: shirts fasten to our backs
and shapes appear lateral and ill-defined.
Dogs hurl themselves into pools
when the requisite conditions are met.

We're all here to have a good time
and get to know each other.

Laughter is measured and occurs in several
continuous instances: here, we are laughing.
There are pineapple slices covered in flies
and we remain endeared toward the simple

animals in our possession.   More dogs, more
dogs, paddling

bellyflop into the neighbor's pool, *Sparky
Pickles, Hunter, Bruce,*

transfixed: dogs displace water
weightlessness, wet, lapping.
See their legs refract at curious and
unnatural angles.

They tread water in the most literal sense.

It is neighbourly to bring finger-food and drinks.
I select wine by the packaging and price tag.

Googling How to be a Motivational Speaker

Ian Goldberg

Begin by skimming the surface,
strip the lacquer off words and their associations.
Squint at fluorescent porch lights, the trembling wrist
the 30 days' notice on the fridge.
Is this what you imagined?

The tyranny of popcorn ceilings?
Finding blood in the mattress liner?
The hands of strangers, knuckle by knuckle
forcing their way under your door?

It's time for a drastic reconceptualisation,
a shot in the arm, *a kick in the ass.*

That's the power of storytelling
the striations of a bullet in motion – spinning.
As a professional truthteller it's evident:
you're FAILING because of you.

It's all in the delivery, the value-add.
It's about reaching people where they are
and inspiring them to be themselves, inspiring them
to pull copper wiring from hotel room fixtures.

In a high conductivity state
you can ambulate without any connective tissue.
It's an act of will, it's nothing.
It's about becoming *nothing*
                            a nothing guru.

All speakers must be motivational.
All speech must be too.

This is a city of *ideas*. You must disrupt the blockchain!
Give public sermons on the virtues of drinking seawater.
Lament how scientology went all *commercial* on us.

It's our fervent belief that sweating needs to be democratised.
Eat a ziplock bag every day – stay fresh, stay limber,
watch six hours of your life slalom into a shallow ditch.

Ask yourself: what will you do?
The present accumulates between molecules,
between the drywall partition. The lights go out
and everything looks brand new.

Adversity is key,   remember that.
      The monitor flickers,   *dims*
folding post-it notes
into   disappearing geometry.

Close your eyes and visualise new levels
of success.
                    Your story is yours and
                  others will pay to hear it.

They will set you free,
cancel all outstanding liabilities.
What an act to follow! Is it everything you imagined?
like strings of light, reaching… dissolving.

It's about reaching people where they are and inspiring them to be you.

Breakfast Buffet

John Son

Holiday Inn, Kensington.
I try to catch Mark's eyes over the jam –
just to spread the transpiration of the moment.

He lifts pans. Hot salty hits of steam
make us blush under the heat lamps.
I quote the unlikely Delia Smith line
and wait for the thunder.

In this place you have to work for the laughs.

Black pudding – enough to conquer
the Isle of Wight. Mark can hear
pointillism from two buildings away
but fails to sublimate sexuality
into what he puts in his morning americano.

No matter, Mark.

Isn't bacon the most nubile of all pork cuts?
Like so much uneaten hollandaise,
I drip coldly onto the Morris rug.

If love were a loaf, it would be thick-cut.
"For longevity."
I surprise even myself, sometimes.
Mark is by the beans, showing serving
staff how to re-contextualise boredom.

Are we continental?
I scoop. Glasses tremble with orange ice.
With my mouth full of egg, I am rakish.
The utensils have been pre-set, Mark –
it's all so refreshing.

Let's turn the spatulas into an advantage.

Let me reheat what's been forgotten.

East of Putney Bridge

John Son

Even after the fact, I continue to dream of men with
a penchant for cufflinks and creme anglaise.

Listen, it was more than just a backhanded fetish. The night
in question was clear: the moon, the lamps, the river,

Max Bemis. What could I say about the north/south
disconnect, the vacancy of the body's cold suburban sprawl?

Your fingers felt like an old acquaintance. The way you
emoted to the ginger biscuits was a throwback.

God, the fridge. Forty more years and I hope I'll be
as fixated with fat free yoghurt as you are.

Maybe I'm not holistic enough. I'm circling back to town
with a smoky sense of a warning, side-benched and two-day

unshowered. Remember how you mummified my legs in your
sheets as an act of pleasure. Remember when I turned away

from you to sleep on the numb part of the bed, what my
refusal to accept father figures did to the toast this morning.

It's bad at Victoria now. Possibly recoil.
Maybe I looked at you too intently when you did what

you did. Maybe I should think about you sweeping
the Fulham Road with a kinder conviction instead.

Am mac mar an t-athair, Peter. Don't you think we'd be better placed looking for gold in amongst the street debris, waiting

for our hands to brush against one another again in those mad, unspeakable moments that sting like burnt spices?

Another restaurant

John Son

At dinner, we ate in line with the concept presented.

I let ravioli, slick with rosemary butter,
slither from my cutlery and onto
bone china, trying to elicit
some canny Italianate mode
of disagreement.

Before we knew each other, this
may have been interpreted as
a protest. Sicilians might have
rallied against our verboten
pine nut- and ricotta-stuffed love.

I felt it most when your legs become
trapped in the joints and jinxes
of your chair and the waiter came
holding a crowbar in gloved hands.
Your napkin became a sign of resilience
in the face of hard times.

We noted that we wouldn't
normally have encouraged this
sort of behaviour.

A squeak of rubber soles as the
sommelier turned to hide his
expression from the table.
New measures were outlined:
inhibiting the emergence of the familial,
redefining collective vernaculars.
The watercolour of Franciacorta
grape vines was repurposed as an
idiom for preservation of the self.

I took potshots at the mortadella.
I tried to identify an exit point
and make ourselves culpable,
question if this was what we really wanted.

Even the osso bucco, slack off the
bone, upset the table and my tongue felt starched
from meditations of romantic legislature.
You, cracking peppercorns onto
the tablecloth, must have felt the sickness
of quickening time in your throat,
the trickle of things yet to be said
stinging nervous pinpricks
on your tongue, twitching your
metal fillings at the nerve.

We continued to amend the certainty
of future agendas.

After closing, they brought us strange courses
that we never ordered and had never
seen on the menu. We tried
to stall and ate reluctantly while
the staff stood lighting cigarettes
in a circle around our table, food
crusting over in half-eaten
plates, my lungs
filling with black smoke.

My Nephew's Second Birthday:
A Saga of Self-Stimulatory Behaviour

Mollie Russell

In three out five

Remember to breathe, says the woman I've never met
as if I could forget, as if her child's party bag had come to life
and wrapped itself around my neck.

In three out five

My sister had dutifully planned the seating arrangement:
his family on the left, ours the right.
   The placard that delegates my space
rests on the lid of the toilet seat, where I spend most of my evening,
avoiding discordant symphonies of children screaming,
bootleg covers of disco hits and phones keening like tinnitus.

In three out five

I am a balloon dressed in black: not in the party mood
Primary pain sears my eyes and plays musical bumps behind the lids
Higher and higher helium sounds stretching my eardrums
   and skin so thin I'm ready to burst

In three out five

into tears. I cannot be the only one crying at a toddler's birthday party.
If I do it over the cake, parents will smoke like party poppers,
the coloured confetti falling out in questions. My relatives will explain,
embarrassed, ashamed, she can't help it, she just gets like this sometimes,

born with a faulty aux cable to her brain,
   the manual was in Swedish, unknown European make,

   In three out five

I am foreign flat packed furniture: frustrating,
when my hands start shaking and my spine starts swaying,
a broken cubicle door, creaking
   and crying an S. O. S: Sensory Overload Sucks,

   In three out five

I am not broken. My bones just need more oiling.
A specialist technician knows exactly where my wires are going.
The neurodivergent can keep going and going,
   faster and further than some standard models,
they just overheat sooner, need more time on battery saver.
Let me let out some air, allow my rubber skin to sag, and stim,
   even if it means I'm floating lower today.

   In three out five

I remember to breathe, no longer having to regulate it manually.
Outside the quiet bathroom sanctuary, the party continues without me.
The candles go out in a single breath, five seconds, no less.

Originally published in The Emma Press Anthology of Illness

Every Woman on Earth Has Won a Razzie for Really, Actually Crying

Mollie Russell

for Shelley Duvall

    Again.
Every sweat-stuck strand is symmetrical on her hairline.
Her throat is swallowed by a beige turtleneck.
The cherub nose is a masterpiece of hours in the makeup department
wept away. She drinks a swimming pool every day.
The camera prowls forward; she backs away, mouth fumbling
to fit around the next line, despite having already said it
one-hundred-and-twenty-five-fucking-times.
    Again.
She rounds the corner, steps like eggshell. Batter up, Shelley. Swing.
The baseball bat's thicker than her forearms.
   She struggles to lift the damn thing.
After, she scoops up a toddler, sprints laps up and down hallways
and lands every step inside a hexagon.
   A fire axe of a man splits his sixtieth door,
and she's sure to thank him for this opportunity, submit
an apology for wasting his time.
    Again.

Flashback to 1977: the final act of *Three Women*.
Fists full of miscarriage, you escape into the dusk.
Your grin swallows scenery. You fill the theatre
with dry, rasping laughter and the click
of your enormous teeth finding their place.
You are a wraith, crimson claws outstretched
towards the camera. Your doe eyes become headlights,
head crowned by the top of the screen
as you come closer and closer, surpass the camera,
never to be captured again.

Originally published in Stone of Madness Press

The Supermarket Night Shift Toasts the Pandemic

Mollie Russell

So, we're ready to do it again:
sit silent on the sofa, sleep in our uniforms
when we return at dawn to our dozing homes.
Because at least the lights are still on.
Because at least we're getting paid.
Because at least the neighbours clapped
for the stability of fourteen-hour days.
Raise a glass for the sanitation of rage
tied to our heads with elastic.
For shovers and spitters and smiles,
the ones that won't wear a mask.
This one's for all the bags. For life
that used to fill my side of the bed.
For my wife, who misses the metronome breaths
that used to fill my side of the bed.
This one's for all the bags for life
and the ones that won't wear a mask.
For shovers and spitters and smiles
tied to our heads with elastic.
Raise a glass for the sanitation of rage.
For the stability of fourteen-hour days.
Because at least the neighbours clapped.
Because at least we're getting paid.
Because at least the lights are still on
when we return at dawn to our dozing homes,
sit silent on the sofa, sleep in our uniforms
so we're ready to do it again.

Death Rattle

Mollie Russell

Change comes slowly / the pinprick light / of a trembling train / on a black horizon / I look away / wait for my eyes to adjust / your lungs become gift wrap / crying out with a crackle when crushed / I creep round the flat in socks / take headphones on and off / on and off / your steps slow / I tell myself you have become more leisurely / with age / your ribs show / pinched by air / I practice / picking up the phone / putting it down again / we kiss goodnight / through tin foil / I strain to form my lips / around that paper-thin truth / how easy it would be to squash this / into a ball / and throw / you fold / over and over / until you are barely there / crunch / when I desperately flatten you / out over the table / my phone lays silent / like a brick / I hold my breath / greedily / stretch / our moments like / the skin of a balloon / your death / rattle vibrates / against the taut face /

Festival

Tom Moody

We have loitered by this portaloo
for days. You tell me about the
novel you are writing and I roll my
eyes like a joint. Are we alike?
You say we are. This area is a
haven for those without inhibitions.

Thank you for cleansing my aura.

Barber's Chair

Tom Moody

Let me practice small talk
before we enter into conversation –

if you wouldn't mind.

My responses are rehearsed.
I have some cracking clichés
in my locker.

Been busy?
Raining again.
Going anywhere nice this year?

Nailed it.

Walsall on a Tuesday

Tom Moody

The bloke with a head like a breeze block leads me through the pub, holding my hand like my mother. The punters, who also have heads like breeze blocks, watch me slot pound coins into the cigarette machine. I am friends with the bloke with a head like a breeze block, and for this reason, the punters, who also have heads like breeze blocks, do not fill me in.

when mercury changed his mind

Rachel Cunningham

for the third time that year, my growth was stunted
and that dangled carrot I hunted, starved of something to gnaw,
saw my naked ponytail stripped of its scrunchie and clawed
its way free

most nights I was suspended, treading water or
skidding aisles over waveless seas,
staining their surface with parallel trails of pale shades like
fingertips on fur stroked tail to head

I would stare at him and wait for the nod
catch cigarette butts between shoulder blades and gaze up as the
engraved lines of his smile started to seep,
hatch plans of stretching to pluck from the clusters of stubble and
using them to hike or cling onto and nuzzle into his pores
    until I was dropped once more

I waited
for the brittle skin around my eyes to grow harder
and stayed still whilst my limbs hid inside casts of salt
hoping for a shift in the wind

waves rode over homes once

Rachel Cunningham

no more
    bubbles of breath from fish lips,
they suckled at leftover salt crystals
and shot their fix of O2 straight into
a cold blood flow, but overdosed on
PVC, and choked when a tsunami of
styrofoam balls and toothbrush bristles
clogged up their gills, and snorkels
built from chewed up starbucks straws

      sunk
           too
                deep

Still Nestlings

Rachel Cunningham

You mustn't think of yourself as a baby bird.
Poised, beak gaping, waiting
For someone's swallowed chunks.
Dwelling on a desire for hollow bones will lead you only where
something ought to have grown, by now.

If you press your brow to glass and squint
the purple sandpiper's grey begins to blend into the sky's tint
you will sigh knowingly at fellow flightless squabs
when their nests grow wide, while you
gulp discarded molluscs until your
body outgrows your mind.

slippery child with wings

Rachel Cunningham

it used to stalk me through bathroom windows
under the gaps in toilet stalls
ducked at tantrum swung doors
spread thin like margarine on piss-stained floor

slid into a spot between un-licked salt rocks
balanced on top of inside-out crisp packets
dabbed at damp spots of drool and
lapped up lingering grease in the crease of its grin

it wore me like a tight pair of jeans
then leapt down my throat head first like two fingers
a sea cucumber formed from the frothy water
of a wave I meant to ride

I stood naked staring back thinking maybe it was god
or the old man from next door

it sipped on my saliva over ice
a slippery child with wings
distracted by my ribs

The Commute

Wendy Falla

Monday morning arrives too soon
we are all
heading for the city, trapped in cars
and railway carriages
silhouettes
leaving our real selves behind, our weekend beings
the ones who have hobbies, go places …
In the mist,
commuters head numbly to the grind
on a fine spring morning.
Daffodils pierce the soil
Snowdrops dip their heads in sorrow
sunrise steams moisture out of the fields
traffic queues at exits, I clock-watch.
Buildings move in ghostlike swathes
or maybe I am moving, not concentrating
as walls begin to swim
I daydream about walking the vicoli of Venice
sipping Aperol Spritz in the shadow of Colleoni
the vista, like a charcoal sketch
shaded with softness
soon left behind
exchanged for the ring road, traffic lights, concrete and car parks
treetops mushroom, bare branch gauzy lace balloons
spinning atop dark column trunks
melded into furrowed earth.
I think of how different the start of day
would have been for my grandfather,
one man, one horse, one plough.

Wild Peacocks

Wendy Falla

Jaspellerie, my childhood home, where peacocks strut,
at dusk they roost on low apple boughs
their magnificent tails draping down like silken scarves.
The path to the door is edged with Calendula and Marigolds.
Old tin roofed house with Rayburn kitchen
heat or hot water, you can't have both.
Rain collected in water butts, boiled before drinking.
A sign in the bathroom reads 'STINK or SWIM'
above a basket of swimsuits to fit all sizes,
wellingtons and raincoats to fit all too.
'There's no such thing as bad weather,' says Grumpa,
'only inappropriate attire,'
a man for all seasons, a man for all reasons,
pop-popping as he sucks on his pipe,
his clothes perforated by cinder burns.
It seems only yesterday we gathered to speak Jerriais
in the kitchen into the small hours,
who died last night and who will be born tomorrow,
drinking tea with milk straight from the cow,
pustules of cream rising to the surface,
Calvados chasers and crumbly sultana Madelaines,
All gone now, all gone …

The Bubble World

Wendy Falla

My mother is lost in a bubble world
cocooned yet vulnerable
she can't remember her name
but can describe the route she took
on her driving test sixty years ago.
She's forgotten how to make tea
but can crochet and knit without patterns.
She confabulates, making up
what she doesn't know.
In convoluted detail she conjures
the life she wanted me to have,
nice home, fictitious husbands,
abundant mythical children,
cute dogs, even happiness.

Symmetry

Wendy Falla

My perfect child
of twenty-seven summers
today
I collected your ashes.
In melancholic symmetry
they weigh exactly
the same as you did
when newborn.

Armbands and Nudity

Sophie Edwards

Estelle can't swim,
but wore a pair of blue trunks anyway.
Everyone stared at her chest
before she was told
never to return to the garden centre again.

Elbow Scab

Sophie Edwards

Estelle picked at her elbow scab
so much it started bleeding.

She grabbed a spoon,
grazed it across her skin
and licked it off.

Tomato Soup

Intercontinental

Sophie Edwards

Like any good daughter,
Estelle thrusts
fried cigarette ends
into her mother's ear.
She then squawks like a goose.

Meal Deal

Sophie Edwards

A pair were caught having sex
by the girl who had a lot of allergies.

After they parted,
Estelle licked the blood left on the sheets

before calling the police.

Nana

Summer Young

Papa's been brushing your slippers for hours
knows your face in snapshots
feels the fur through his fingers like a child

a doe wakes up, finds a baby in the straw that is hers

Nana you look so tired – curled pink shell
in a bouquet of duvet
I bake fairy cakes for you, your own recipe
smear buttercream over your blue lips to revive you
Papa scrapes the bowl clean with a single finger,
remembers your wedding day, loses the image

a stone in a crooked heart shape
falls through the lining of an old coat

I'll always be your Little Girl in a Norfolk twang
It's not the same, drawing circles
on my own palm
beautiful black and white on a swing in Barbados
Papa's favourite photo of you

Shut up, bite down

Summer Young

I want bones, rattle
on the top deck of the 43
drawing yourself into restaurants
in a picture where the plate is perfectly 2D

bones at Halloween, long white lines
inhaled

& painted over tracing paper skin
always choose skeletons, dance
with Beth round the fire like Funny Bones
our beautiful bodies clanking as we mould them
into the most inhumane silhouettes

& the fire never really warms you, does it?
leaves fall over your grey bodies
laid to rest on the wet grass & woken
by morning sun cutting through cold cheeks

Writings from Spain

Summer Young

and there's this big slice of watermelon in his lap.
he sucks the flesh as he stares

— the bulls are a fair fight
& they're hard as nails —

the television only speaks Spanish. Somewhere
he spits pips at lizards with their tails off
they patter so loud

The fifth spear,
      the sixth.
popped, the bull deflates —
it is huffing, or he is,
or we have all let out a collective sigh.
one thing certain —

it is done

*

on all our fingers there's this stickiness.
when you watch your father in rage
you breathe through your sweater sleeve.
It is a heavy censorship and it tires you

before the bull is released for the fight
it is half-blinded and beaten.
some see death coming and bow their heads.
He — father — he mocks

– you thought you could stomach (it/me/this) –
I didn't hear
over bulls' bodies punching the sand
there was one and there was one hundred and they all looked to me
for tips on salvation.   I was nine

> *Bull, my hands soften for you. my name and all its connotations*
> *would be sanctuary   and I'd love you.   if only I could*
> *reach you*

*

I woke this morning and put on a red fleece
so he sees I have bled too
or is it that I need for him to stay untrusting
so I dress as the matador

*

I was only little once, and I found these baby birds
fresh from the egg and mother warned
not to taint their scent but
in the morning   it was so early
and mother slept
and father lifted me up by the armpits

and I tainted them all.   – tiny, bony things.
he did it for me
or did it to spite her.   or he'd always been this way
not that it fucking matters
in the night / the mother bird / screams / so loud
& I wake up   in a bloated body

*

This isn't really about Spain at all –

I am so sorry
to have deceived you

A Manifesto on Existing and Expiring

Ellie Sparks

you make me want to die / but i'm still alive / and isn't that the point? / my mum says i should write an inspirational tweet / or a self-help poetry book / but i plucked this survival from luck / just like i did before / i am no user manual / how about i take my own experience / and refuse to ram it down your throat? / i can imagine you've been clogged / ever since you made pinkie promises with your own psyche / and forgot to slather the melancholy all over your body / just to slumber in it / and perish / the world needs more people like me / apparently / and i've been trying to figure out what that really means / and whether it's possible to exist and expire both at the same time / i guess i'm no plath / i like to watch that happy ending unfold like a silk sheen / stencil petals over my skin like i'm an ornamental corpse / only, will that happy ending ever come to me / if i lose my head / over being subjected to locker room threats? / will i be able to taste the sun / without first licking the dew / from the lacerations you've left atop my skin? / will i be able to watch my termination / if my survival is dependant upon contingency? / i guess all of this ponderation is just manifestation of a sticky salty end / a funeral no-one wants to attend / i guess my permanence is just a tumbleweed.

Mad Woman

Ellie Sparks

Don't you dare tell me
I can't be angry
when you've spent
an entire lifetime
swallowing me and
trapping me inside
your chest.
I just want a cavity
of my own,
bones I can click into place.
I don't want to
fester beside your
curling flesh.

Lost Cause

Ellie Sparks

Maybe I should understand
by now
why everything I learn to love
learns to leave me mutilated.
My grandma says it's
a wise thing
to break up with ardour
before it lacerates me,
but I don't think she
realises my limbs
are disjointed and cracking
like the sacrum of her spine,
my sternum is
malfunctioning into a
mechanical claw, and
the chambers of my
heart are inhaling arsenic
and exhaling venomous nitrates.
How do I tell her
I'm already a human sacrifice?
How do I tell her
I can already see the plank
stretching out before me?

Let's Christen This Sin of Ours

Ellie Sparks

If you are Orion, I am your nebula / your chapped core / your malted middle / I know you've tried to extradite me from your soul / before I've had the desire to jump twenty light years from your chest / but you have to understand / that we're both part of this barely baptised belt now / we're both meshed into a volcanic mould / a luminous lesion / and now we're compressed / christening this sin of ours is going to make this constellation burst / into a sort of star dew that famishes the celestial sphere / eats the ether inflammable.

Spectrum

Stephen Mizen

Your life is a spectrum
each moment a miracle of being
but yours to control and change

it might seem strange
but you are not a child, a wild creature
taught to be tame,
but that same distain for blame
brought you there
then here.
Here where you couldn't have been years ago
where dreams are possibilities coming true

Because you are you
and the more you do the more you will find
the best moments of your life repeat with the same bassline
and that bassline is just
your cosmically gorgeous mind.

The Stardust that ended us as your mirrors image
is no-one's imagination
so why not have fun?

You're in control of your destiny
not her, or him, or we
you
so go and do whatever your good soul wants to
go kill all the demons
and ride all the dragons
and never be afraid to be flagging
because to be anything less

is to be everything less
and what mess it is to be less then
stardust, and splendour, and
you
So I'll say it again so it gets through
you can do whatever the high heaven you want to.

Utopia's a hard place to find,
and utopia's a hard place to define
but utopia can be yours and mine
if you just walk   your own bassline

Ramshackled

Stephen Mizen

Draw me another stratosphere
with that dreamer intoxicating soul
and whilst I map out the route
pour me another glass
make it smooth dark and clear
we can drink it here

They say ramshackled,
but we know what it means to be at
the bottom of a barrel
we just twist that thing on its side
they think we're going downhill
we're just finding the quickest way to the river, babe.

And as we bob downstream
navigating through those same
dream intoxicating stars
you can point out all the poetry bars
and I'll give off the mirage
the fine façade
that I'm the one in charge.

A Haiku

Stephen Mizen

A Haiku? Bullshit
Bullshit Bullshit Bullshit Bull-
Poetry is great

Tigeress

Stephen Mizen

They say there's a place in Thailand
where if you're feeling brave enough
you can walk up and touch a chemically tamed tiger
the beast of Bengal dosed into submission
stripes vibrating above a sedated, drug hungry heart
waiting for the next nullification from its keepers

And yet I see you Tigeress
impossible to ignore, your roar,
somehow louder than before
strong yet cautious, you move and I see it
Orange, black flames.

Dead skin is a medal to hunter
the same as silenced beauty to a social climber
neither see their rewards in its glory days
instead both strip prizes bare
until all that left is a shell
that used to solider of mind
a warrior of beauty.

The Hunters came for Tigeress, they craved you
and gave you what they thought
you ought to desire
but all I see now are the emptying eyes
teeth obvious in a sagging mouth but for the first time
not dangerous just
fucked

Before you get tied to a post and tourist come for you
I'll rouse you
come alive lady Shere Khan
get mad, fury,
roar
chase me and bite into my flesh so I know you're alive

5 Things I Wish You Knew

Summer Bramall

1. I still cross the street to avoid men walking towards me. Especially when it's dark.

2. I still hold my breath when I hear people arguing.

3. I still look for your approval from nearly every man I meet.

4. When the professor in my first ever poetry class asked us to write about our earliest memory, I had to lie. Somehow, telling a roomful of people I had just met about how my mother's face looked as you bashed her skull into the wall didn't seem too appropriate.

5. When you left, and I never saw you again, I learnt that the people you love won't always love you the way you want them to, if at all.

Clinomania

Summer Bramall

(n.) excessive desire to stay in bed

Sleep eludes me.
Sleep is but a walking shadow
who is always one step ahead.
Sleep's perfume clings to me like a desperate child,
but she herself is nowhere to be found.

The clock titters at my insomnia.
He knows Sleep will not come when I call her,
but rather,
will allow me to toss and turn,
searching for her.

It is only when the night has run out
that she will appear at my fingertips.
Sleep looks at me with pleading eyes
as the alarm blares like a siren.
Stay, she whispers, undressing –
and before I reply,
her lips put me under.
She envelops me, and I breathe her in,
as the morning light streams in through the window.

A Chronology of Kisses

Summer Bramall

Just before these lips were kissed for the first time,
I held my breath,
so the butterflies in my stomach didn't escape.
I was sweating so much
I thought we would drown.
He tasted like he was already gone.

The last time these lips kissed,
there was no panic-induced shiver down my spine,
no bone-chilling
'oh-god-he's-going-to-kiss-me' moment,
no sweaty palms, no aching, no shaking,
no flurry of butterflies
threatening to make me vomit on his shoes.
Instead,
we melted into each other
like butter on a hot stove.

He kissed me like he hadn't eaten in days,
but there was no hunger there.
After all, you cannot lust after something
you know is yours.

And the next time these lips kiss,
we will toast marshmallows with the warmth of our love.
I will feel safe in its simplicity,
as he will taste like he sees me
with all my flaws and imperfections
and will gladly stay longer.

The First Witches

Summer Bramall

The first witches did not fly brooms.
They spent long hours knitting sticks to defend themselves
against men who would beat them regardless.

The second generation of witches realised
how powerful their mothers had become,
and discovered
they could, in fact,
fly.

Train tracks

Sarah Standage

No holiday
Yellow star

Interminable
Crammed, chaotic cattle trucks
Difficulty breathing
Shit scared
Stench
Doors – locked
Windows – barbed wire

Hungry
Thirsty
Faint
Condemned to starve
No talking
Cheeks wet
Nagging dread
Relentless journey
Fear

*Day into night into day into night into day
into night into day into night into day into*

A stolen life
No hope
No possessions
No hair
Propelled towards
A number

Wrong future

No education

Sarah Standage

I mused on the word that rhymes with duck
Littered in our speech
So many words in the English language
and some rely on this one

Said repetitively it loses its effect
Starts to reflect on the user
On the page it ceases to shock
Becomes tedious
Lacks imagination.

And then I read
Evidently Chicken Town.

It was fucking brilliant
It fucking rhymed
With fucking rhythm
I fucking understood
His fucking mind
His fucking descriptions
His fucking need to escape
His fucking desperation
His fucking life.

Cabbage Aisle Kids

Imogen Cook

Supermarkets remind me of marriage.
You're my fifth wife. You don't even know it.
Carry broccoli down the cold white aisle
like a bouquet of green static flowers.

In the car park lies a stranger's omen –
rain-soaked condom, suggestion of absence.
They could have called the baby Aldi.
I think about Aldi for hours.

I want Aldi with you. Or with someone.
You want Brooklyn. India. No-one.
There's a plane ticket under your mattress.
There's a plastic doll lodged in my womb.

Supermarkets remind me of marriage.
Supermarkets remind me of you.
Supermarkets are gateways to hospital wards.
I'll find you at the check-out. Soon.

Frankenstein

Imogen Cook

Until 1am I was reading
Frankenstein in the library,
learning what a lack of
love can do to a body, and
on the way home I am
surrounded by drunks and
their caretakers for a long while,
some hand in hand, others
crawling into long black cars:
eventually, they disintegrate, smile
or cry into darkness, and I am left
in the almost alone two long dark streets
from home. A man has walked behind me
for five or six hundred yards now
and I quicken my pace when he does,
tighten my grip on the keys between my
fingers, try not to look over my shoulder
too many times; I feel bad letting him know
I mistrust him, that this silence shared
with a stranger feels less like peace and more
like menace. I can't stop thinking about
Frankenstein. Dear God, I'm thinking, I hope
someone has loved that body of his,
saved mine.

Birds

Imogen Cook

I love birds the best but a sparrow flew
before me on the path
and my heart leapt through
my skin, beat against the gravel –
I knew then I'd gone too far
on an empty stomach.
I've been walking for years
trailing invisible dogs through the mud,
telling myself not to fear
my many uglier twins, the ghosts,
the tall boys on their bikes.
Not to punish any of them –
it's been a long winter and they tried
their best to find food under dirt.
Still, sometimes my legs feel too light
for my chest. Sometimes I want to fight them,
kick back with these lace-up boots, hurt
something, anybody, nobody. The birds
do not make so much sound,
float past with their light bodies
like cobwebs in wide kitchens
and still I tremble like a caught child.
"Does that make sense to you?" I ask
nobody in particular. I could walk forever,
go round in island-circles and convince
myself I'm escaping the stranger
in my clothes. I turn back eventually
and hide at home. I peck at mashed potatoes
whilst the sparrows eat forkfuls of heart,
their tiny beaks scraping, barely-heard,
against the hard round pebbles.

the you is plural

Imogen Cook

i check twitter to procrastinate peeling off my jeans / i've been having recurring dreams about running from nuclear bombs / into endless basements like a skyscraper turned upside down / last time i was in town / you told me i was right to hate your ex-boyfriend / i didn't know how to explain that i hate being right more / every time a writer i like commits suicide via wikipedia page / i feel like i'm falling down a great elevator shaft / into the skyscraper upside down / all the floors gutted out / remember world war three / how when you and i kissed in that too-crowded bar / some old american man was watching / YOU MAKE SUCH A LOVELY COUPLE / i never saw you again / answered your texts without further questions / we were his more than ours / you fell from a great height the year i was born / your wedding photos were beautiful / and i don't know what to do with the clothes you gave me / when you and i and you and i and you and i and you and / i reach the bottom floor of the country / and it is dark and sticky like a disused nightclub / i lace my fingers between yours / say since i know we're about to die / i really fucking liked you / as if it's an insult

To the lemur underneath my bed

Molly Penney

Are you nocturnal?
You must be.
I only ever hear you at night.
You scratch at the slats and claw at the ends of my sheets
until I pull back.
Are you checking up on me?
Are you making sure I haven't suddenly died?
I used to get scared like that too when I shared a room.
My sister would be breathing and then boom –
   the room would go silent,
so I'd lie awake thinking is she dead?
And I'd make a noise, I'd clap or something,
and she would stir, or gurgle, or sometimes
   she would look at me and scowl,
she thought I was waking her up to be mean.

Her eyes were hard to see in the dark but yours are gorgeous,
they're like fruit,
two small glowing fruits, round and beating.
Your pupil is black though, dead centre,
like I have x ray vision,
like I can see straight into the fruit at its core,
at its pip.

You never scowl at me, but you don't look happy either,
I suppose you are probably a long way from home.
It says here you are from Madagascar,
it looks warmer there.
Don't worry, tomorrow I will buy you a blanket.

Blessed

Kaycee Hill

Over breakfast the Devil came to me,
belching sulphur all over my porridge.
Big bristled hooves, forked tongue,
three blinding breasts – heavy, round,
the shade of koff candy twists.

She offered me a one-eyed lamb's head,
tight-lipped clam shells, a box of tampons.
Her nipples cracked into a map
of Southampton, leaked honey,
melted the cutlery.

She squeezed the flaming teat in an antique
goblet, mixed it with tears then slid it
across the table – *drink me* – etched
into its base. She tasted sweet
like girlhood,

peppered with a musk I had tasted before:
my first experience with death
when Play died, finding unused needles
buried inside window ledges,
red inside white cotton,

smeared up the middle like roadkill.
Her flavour frenzied every bud,
like ants spewing wings, taking flight.
I felt one hundred hymens breaking
like bird skulls,

tumescence of hips swelling to the ocean,
the smell of Golden Virginia,
baked tarmac, lemon Shake n' Vac,
taste of Parma Violets, crayons,
microwaved milk.

Through this mirage I saw mountains
of bubblegum taffeta, clear princess
tiara gems, Anne Frank's diary –
dog eared, hair stuffed into Bic razors
and my first big-girl bedroom.

Care Bears stood to attention on entry,
all white tummies, fat and full.
And my old rocking horse restored
to glory, exactly how I kept her,
with the bridle removed,

a box stood in the nucleus of the room,
inside it smelt like pencil shavings, lilies,
stay here forever, the Devil said –
brushing my hair with one coiled paw,
as the goblet topped itself up.

I took a sip, kneaded into her lap
and let sleep take me,

locusts fell from her cheeks,

the sun laboured a look.

The Collector

Kaycee Hill

She comes to me, every night
at the stroke of three, well fitted in her
black and her white, to greet me.

She taps twice, two for joy –
with her pointed matte, black beak
and drops from her tongue
treasure, onto my window sill.

She brings flecks of silver foil, beads
from necklaces passed, beer
coloured glass and sometimes when
she is feeling generous, gold.

She is a strange creature, beautiful in
her plumage, her ink blue tail-stripe
winking as she turns to feed, I
am certain she likes me watching her.

She eats her fill and when she is done
shoots her beady, liquid topaz eye into
mine and flies into the shrieking wind.

Polystyrene Cup

Kaycee Hill

Once, we drove to the nature reserve
and watched from our seats, as frogs went
piggybacking from pond to pond.

I dropped my polystyrene cup out the
window. It was scarred with fingernail indents
and lipstick bruises

You bust-a-gut laughing as it melted

The radio fidgeted with static

Scuffing

Kaycee Hill

after Maya Angelou

I picture my mother at eleven years old –

      bowlegged, pint-sized, confined in her uniform,
eyes weary even then, pulled in at the corners,
          cast in hickory, flecked with gold,

      the same shade Diana Ross and The Supremes wore
on the cover of *Cream of the Crop*, shook those hips in,

gappy teeth, freckled cheeks, walking home from school,
dragging new Clarks against salmagundi brick,

their leather-cracked cry trailing behind
      like the music of a cabassa made from gourd,
like bay leaves laughing, rice and peas boiling.

I see her enjoying the scuffing, revelling in its wrongness –

the desecration of shoes so foreign, so hideous,
      her mouth flung open to the sky like Maya's,
armed to the back teeth with glee

(that pot of Kiwi black polish under the sink, that'll slide over
the damage like shea butter).

      We need much less than we think we need
          did Mum consider that?

Did a guilt-seed bloom, nestled between mince roly-poly,
mash and veg, coiling like bantu knots?

I see her playing out the trouble she'd be in, hearing it
like an echo in an aluminium can,
great-nanny's voice rearing up

over the ruins, the crime scene,

then simmering down to a tiny puff of steam
because she's eleven, grown, a God –

This House That I Cling To

Rebecca Ward

Time has abandoned this house that I cling to
Like the humans long before.
They used to run barefoot across the grass
laughing, with cheeks as pink as my petals.

But time has abandoned this house that I cling to
Like the glass fled windowpanes
when the fire swept throughout my walls
and burnt my roots to ash.

Time has abandoned this house that I cling to
And Time has abandoned me, too.
My branches are brown and brittle
Crumbling, like this house that I cling to.

Apple

Laura McKenzie

She sat on a crate
watching them bring in the harvest,
russet globe gobleted in hand.

It pleased her:

taught flesh waxed skin-to-skin,
classical, grand;

how burdened trees crooked their waists,
bent to the stretch of the labourer's claw;

that chomp and slurp and zing and fizz,
teeth mulching to the core.

She tossed her fruity grenade skywards, laughing,
catching
another perfect year.

Circus

Laura McKenzie

Trapeze Man
Hot Shot
In Air
Big Front
Flip Flop
Wrist Lock
Knuckles White
Your Delight
Hawkeye
In Command
Trust Me
Superman

On Ground
Trouble Bubble
Spilling Over
Kids Wife
Dead Life
Heart Ache
All Break
Pieces
On Floor

In The Park

Laura McKenzie

Today I am I and you are you.
        We are us.
Today we sit in the park
        and watch the ducks.
Today you kiss me and I love you.
Today the pond is still,
        there is colour
        and bread.
Tomorrow will come.
Tomorrow will cry.

        Tomorrow you'll leave.

Sylvia

Laura McKenzie

You are not you, you are not you
anymore, dead
oven head, little onion
peeling
back back back
to an iron ore
pure as your eye

You tried to die, three times, four?
the thrill, the spill of life,
a wife at Primrose Hill,
lover, mother, basket
case of the blues

The news hit hard for you,
Ted in bed with the witch
bitch,
and you a smiling mannequin
carted off to Belsen
yanking out the telephone
casting off your Daddy clone

to the sin bin,
love's thin, paper feel
shivering
palely, fraily as your asphyxiated lung,
hung like a ham hock,
strung out for the dead poet society and
feminist flock

And I, fifty years too late
to rescue you.
Sylvia,
I will never be through.

Behind Quarantine Doors

Eden Irving

As I stare out of boarded-up window holes,
contemplating from my quarantined berth,
I fantasise the interactions I'm missing right now.
Feelings unshared, thoughts internalised for eternity,
conversations left on the cutting room floor.
Society's runaway train lost control atop closed borderlines,
flinging us, loose debris into the danger zone.
Collateral damage in the hands of fate.
Roll up, roll up! Hand in your Costas, give up your Maccie D's,
readjust to a diet of cookies, pot noodles
    and water by the conservative gallon.
We're in times of contradiction in a world of conflated facts:
you take care by shutting out,
go out to be alone,
be alone to save others
yet be blinded to others through isolation
    more extroverted than anyone it's tainted.
But it means nothing, does it?
Not until the mass graves get dug next door.

Punching my Paradox in the Face

Eden Irving

I don't need to creep into the changing rooms, but I do.
Not so I don't rouse beasts of unbridled banter
  and hormonal rage around me, no.
I'm an intruder.
My mask? A slanted jawline and several dozen
  twiddly strands of hair south of the neckline.
Plus, you know, the obvious genital outliers.
Dart past the racks of rucksacks and coats into the cubicle.
It's rank. It's cramped. It's horrific.
It'll do.
I wanna faze into the brickwork, into my own private quarters.
The bog shall suffice.
Layers of clothing unpeel to reveal the invisible schoolyard wounds.
I view life through a Facebook filter.
It's real but it's warped, edited…wrong.
I pass my days with this broken app,
  unable to waft the aerosol out of my vision.
That's why I keep looking down,
  eyes planted on the cracks in the pavement.
There's no mirrors in them. No reflections or stinging realities.
Just my feet, carrying on. Keeping up the pace.
Avoiding my Frankenstein Monster complex.
I don't recognise my smile.
Teacher's calling, boys yelling as they leap
  into action on the football field.
They can live without me.
I realise this now. Years after those school days of listlessness.
Heart and mind merely making do
  with the little apartment they're renting out.
But the past is in the past, locked in a scrapbook.

Sealed recollections I can only handle
    when the planets align and my world feels…decent.
Dip back in to remember freeze-frame shots of nostalgia.
Gazing eyes meet my own in the pocket mirror and I pause.
Food for thought? Try a banquet.
One I have to gorge it every time before
    I can continue my day in relative comfort.
I am a paradox.
I am true, but this…my vessel of truth is false. It's not me. But it is…
Paradoxical quandaries fuel questioning to come in adulthood.
Fears, fury, ounces of euphoria giving me glimpses,
    chances, glances at happiness.
I imagine said happiness.
And I know I will thrive.
I imagine coming out to friends, family,
    strangers in the street without a second thought.
And I know I will thrive.
I imagine the validation, the affirmation,
    the trust in ones I choose to let know.
I imagine the first steps to take, and the next,
    and the…well, the last will never come.
Transitioning with each passing day
    into a me who can give more, go farther.
A chemical reaction gone wrong in all the right ways.
And I know I will thrive.
If I were to go back, I'd find a mirror.
Better understanding the fog and filters I'm staring into,
    let the water settle around me.
I stare at the paradox that is my birth, my past,
    my body – knowing it doesn't have to be me.

And I PUNCH it!
And I tell the dysphoria to fuck off!
And I tell the morons who called me weird
 and strange and stupid to get fucked!
And I tell myself that I don't have to accept stereotypes
 and styles as set in stone.
That the dissatisfaction, the confusion,
 the feeling of the in-between has a name.
That I'm allowed to say 'fuck it!'
 and be someone I'll enjoy being tomorrow.
And when I know I will thrive, I smile.
For that's all I need to get there.

we are in Disneyland eating a fry up
and all I can think about is death,

Beth Phillips

ie, I am seventeen and probably too old to be here with my parents.
& the fast-track tickets for *it's a small world* are wasted
when you have forgotten how to queue.
& woody doesn't seem to be having as much fun
without buzz.

 I have a reoccurring nightmare that all my stuffed toys come alive
& sew my limbs together. I am thrown down the stairs in a duffle bag.
                    the next morning visitors step over my body
                before admiring the gallery wall in the hallway.

ie, mom slams her fork as the buffet opens.
she smuggles tiny jams into her pocket for me to snack on.
& im taking a holiday from being overwhelmed by textures.
& im scared she'll take me back to april house
if I don't look like im having fun.

                         the first meal out together tasted like limbo.
                          I prayed no one knew it was my birthday,
                  ordered noodle salad because it's a safe option.
                        we both cried in the car on the way home.
                           she asked why I was withdrawn
                       but all I could think about was showering.

ie, it's been a month since her last trip to out of hours
& we weren't sure if her lungs would handle the flight.
& I don't speak much french and don't understand
health insurance but the receptionist told me
what to do in an emergency.

her skin is sore from light treatment,
blister stains dancing up her chest. & we talk about cancer
as a friend. she will repeat stories of sneaking off the ward
to try and find me. moments later, she is gagging on morphine.

we are still in Disneyland and I have just finished breakfast.
I wonder if I died here, would they cancel the firework display?

pumpkin

Beth Phillips

on saint catherine's hill the light looks like a memory,
where the stretch of sun teases us into stripping off.
we sip punch on the hilltop
      until we feel sick,
plaiting curls and painting skin
with fingerprints. on the way home we jump
over chapel gates,
share pastries,
      wipe cherry stains from our lips.

when we reach the patio you play vienna.
I hold your hand from the hammock, head resting
on my stomach as we wait
for the gate to open,
for our friends to find us
      beautiful and steaming.

lourdes

Beth Phillips

and on sunday you spoke to god   and he asked why you had given up on faith

but how do you tell the lord that his teaching has turned bitter   that there is no joy

in eating a meal   if you cannot take pleasure in the preparation

and now you live closer to dying than survival   everything you touch cannot be felt

a certain numbness that erodes   where do your hands begin   you make no sudden movement

when you walk the ground thinks you're a fallen leaf or a lost child

you've lost all strength to reach the top floor without feeling breathless

perhaps this is the distribution they warned you of   but you are still pot-bellied

with bug-like limbs

and they will tell you it's easier to swallow and forget

but everything inside you is the same

sit in one room waiting for prayers

girls like you meet on a friday morning   and the walls have a funny charm

ask permission to the bathroom where everything is sterilised   an emptiness

you smile at the holes   your hands   where water cannot be felt

you search for more than most things

that is what lauren asks when you meet

why is there this space that you wish to no longer take

but you cannot tell this doctor   who you now think is god   that there is no point

in being who you are meant to be when you look different in every reflective surface

when you cannot pull away from each feature   and the stairs get further away

the more you try to meet the sky

and still

Beth Phillips

she is hunched over a bucket,
spewing bright lights in the living room.

men countdown the distance between door / and bucket /
        she looks at me like I am nameless.
the room will groan for more time as she is lifted from the sofa.
and this leather is all consuming / hugging onto thighs /
she will tell me she is thirsty and all I can find is sorry

dad unlocks the gate
wheels her through glass.
I am the only one that can see her.

she reverses off the drive / god save the stillness /
when the evening is mute
I am in your arms.

Digital Chicken Gravy

Jack Stacey

I reopened a forgotten thought from my computer;
only place left to hide.

Best not talk about private stuff
with ink or pencil,
or sporadic voice fossilised on a tree.

Yes, I opened the computer,
read the holy grail crap from my brain,

the recycled unhappiness
from said date and time,
sitting there like the old castle ruin
people pay to visit.

What does it say you ask?
If I told you this before
you'd probably not care.

I tell my digital therapist instead.
She has a digital name and tons of digital wisdom.
She tells me there's lots to live for.
I told her my thought:
There are fewer butterflies around.
She said some things only exist when you're a child.

What happens when enough of us snuff it?
All those digital graveyards,
those names and faces and photos.

There'll be no more room in digital hell.
Zombie group chats will walk the empty streets.
That'll be the best horror that ever lived.

My Ball of Yarn Thinking

Jack Stacey

I decided to kidnap the Sun.
I wouldn't use it for my own benefit,
I'd keep Sun in one of the spare drawers under the bed –
no one looks there.

Keep people away from the Sun, I say.
Keep them from their happiness,
fake happiness causing surreal body odour in their brains.
Make people listen to the clouds
give clouds time to explain themselves.

Fuck, I just want a burger right now.
Streamline fat, salt and succulence, with a mouthful of ale
and tell everyone how I'm gonna 'half-inch the Sun.'
But no one cares. Not really.

Tomorrow in a Teabag

Jack Stacey

Hello, I said,
to anything listening
whilst on my walk in the bare woods
of one of my dreams.

I try to talk in my sleep as often as possible.
They say it's good to stay connected.
These bare woods:
recent rainfall and fog,
the ice cold slathered on my nose-tip
exhuming the multiple fir trees'
and their reek of Jesus' birth.

I'm rubbing my eyes in these woods.
Found a random cliff edge with a painted view below.
This view is going to kill me, I say.
Right ol' rainforest, looks like an ocean of broccoli.
I dove in – dunno why, that's just what dreams make me do.
Etcetera's of life were all over the place.

I wanna take a hot flannel over everything,
rub away those greasy spots that curse our
tearful pubic faces.

Random Access Memories

Jack Stacey

My old cafe uses funky slate coasters for my coffee from Brazil
and has funky, modern art chairs made of plastic
and wood painted blue, with funky designs
but its legs don't screech a 'daft punky sound'
and they never play *Da Funk* by Daft Punk.
But this boy walks in
who wears daft punky clothes
who weighs about half a funky slate coaster,
brings his own wooden chair –
        and orders a water and a Twix.

I lay awake that night
thinking about that fuckable cake
that oozed its sugary charm
all in my face.

Pirouette

Sophia Georghiou

All I care about is a hairy Italian man in shorts and his comedy wife.
I down white wine, watch him slice open
a packet of frozen prawns and chuck them into a pan.

He joins me on the sofa to *talk first*, begins by telling a story
about the reputation he once had. The pan spits
Those pills guys put in girls' drinks, I've never needed to use those.

I sit tight legs stiff, the way we were taught in ballet.
Focus on his story that has now drifted into a new one
about cars or cycling to work.

He stands up like he's about to make an announcement,
unzips, and spits in his palm.
Fits the other around the back of my neck, I close my eyes.

The way to pirouette is to perfect your spotting technique,
relaxing the neck, focusing the eyes,
and whipping the head.

Breathe and float around in your turn,
remember that it is not a spin,
but a controlled up and down movement, like drawing a circle.

After he comes, he wipes a strand of hair from my chin.
I push past and bow into the kitchen sink.
I needed that, he breathes. *I'm hungry, let's eat.*

Autumnal

Jamie Cavallo

A child's sweatshirt, left hanging on a cemetery gate
Hand-knitted in shades of pumpkin and chestnut threaded
loosely around the rusted, gothic spikes
Watching as the old oaks shed tears of a nearing winter.
Its sleeves bleed where the hungry moths feed and where the
whinchats rests before he proceed
Curious harvest mice gaze up with interest, wondering
why something so pure, so lively, would be left with the dead.
As the spiders let their webs speckle with icy dew
does it feel useless?
As the costumed sprites trick and treat, does it long
for skin and warmth?
Has it ever felt skin and warmth?
In shades of pumpkin and chestnut,
it waits for the snow to fall

Under my bed I watch
my wall partially collapse

Henry Donald Marks

From my *NEIDEN* crawlspace I peer through wet, slotted fingers.
Dribbling plaster spilling, peeling lather bubbles from acne drywall.
Filaments twinge and hang from the fallen brick,
earth and live spark alike before returning to a placid shadow.
Volcanic jazz-hands worming as darkness drawls,
His spine scorched, Nagasaki silhouette on brickwork.

Under bare lattice beams, screaming termites covet their missing shade.
Their Western Wall has been soaked with pesticide.

Pinholes of LED, acid yellows and migraine pinks,
Throbbing through a hundred gasping portholes.
their pungent bulbs murmur and zip, growling like humbugs,
drilling outwards, violating the greyscale limbo.

the taste of strange new breath cartwheels in.
Inhaler squeeze,
puff, pull,
It sounds the same, but it isn't mine.
   My inhaler is brown with a yellow cap, and sounds like

CzhhIK – shhhheeee

It's not my inhaler, and It's coming from the ceiling,

Salbutamol halitosis cloud trudging,
hacking and hammering down from behind the attic door
retching, heavy smells, the unwashed microwave fans,
the fungal yeast-flavoured belch of my alcohol-soaked mouth.
the grey weeping smog tumbles feet first down my fire-exit stairs.

oesophageal encounters of the third kind,
   tractor beamed my red body skyward
upwards and further into oxygen deprived outlines.
unhooked from my sleep apnoea machine I wail
grunting into pixilated Primark bedding
chanting the anaphoric Om between bleak autumnal sobs,
seized in tinnitus blaring lamp-light, reeling
fish-hooked, line rigid on the verge of snapping
Catherine-wheel of best-before asparagus stench,
shivering, cornered by a madhouse of beetles.

Vanity Wing

Henry Donald Marks

I've been shaving my arm hairs from the skin.
In the mirror I am Marilyn Monroe's dry forehead,
   crackling corpse pork-husk.
The fuzz of my armpit drops in tessellated imperfection
   onto my Volkswagen carpet.
When you're repulsive, you're a weapon.

     I'm the potential kinetic energy you see humming and
     sparking in static visual disturbances against the air just
     breaths before a terminal road-traffic collision.
     I'll be rinsed and dry, just give me ten. There will be no hair
     left by the time I get to Hayling Island.

A rushed swipe of the plastic held blade snags,
tugging into my fibula, anchored to my open bone.
Yelping, I blow and fan cold air into my wound.
Thirty meters in less than a second.

     And then there's Mr. President,
       Jackie and the twins, paused in their
     motorcade, just six meters from my bonnet.
       In a millisecond I'll be
     the vehicular Lee Harvey Oswald.

     I hammer the unyielding brake with my heel,
       hurling my pulsing,
     kidney-bean knuckles to the handbrake.
       My blonde hairs have
     clumped and packed the pedal.

before the impact my feet split through the belly of Kurt.
I tumble through the dual-carriageway, dropped from the bomb doors,
roadkill flashes by my neck as I spin, barrelling down further,
    scraping earth's mantle on the roof of my mouth
I spill, hurtling onto the bedroom floor of a man
He looks just like me, pure.

Checking for Elijah

Henry Donald Marks

The Animated Haggadah angel of death
plasticine fever dream –
eye bogies flesh out the stacked Afikomen crunch,
teeth chafe on the dry density of five-pound sterling between cousins
and grandparents and parents and soaking wet glances –
micro granules of matzo meal wad
  extendable dining-table cracks with stale slavery,
washed down in the bitterness of kiddush wine,
Elijah eludes another seder,
peace be upon you or peace be with you, when peace
strikes your mezuzah and flies over the slanted
dartboard of a doorframe with a sickle in his arm and
a gasping spectral jaw, sniffing for lambs' blood
and the shivering of skull caps under extendable dining- tables.
Holy Moses!

Head's droop and backs recline to the left,
and wheezing ephemeral rifts in the evening treeline circle the first star
Holy Moses!
He's coming out of the woodwork,
Holy Moses!
Hellish witch of special agency,
hardly a heavenly body,
cracking spinal glockenspiel
nick-nacking night-wind blowing in the ribcage of Lilith,
whistling wishbone panpipes trill klezmorim scales
     amongst lost muscle sinews
and the hollow woodwind fingerings of an ashen Ashkenazi,
Putrid, teary, bellowing: 'Adonai, leave me alone!'
Holy Moses Great Hoary Morph Clay-Mation
     Angel of Death and Hate-Crimes and Race Wars!
Holy Moses, Holy Elijah, leave me to rot,
faithless.

Letters for you

Olivia Sinthathurai

I wrote to you with confessions of love,
And never heard a word

I wrote to you giving you my time,
But you drove away to work

I wrote to you a list of my favourite places
And you laughed knowing the truth

I wrote to you my devotion
But you scoffed in my face

I do not love, you said and shut the door
And I opened it to never let you go.

Lessons from my first night away from home

Lawrence Nicholas

1. Nothing smells right.

2. This bed is not my bed
   no matter how well
   I cocoon myself in it.

3. I think I'm going to like my flatmates;
   they're not talking to me like a wheelchair.

4. Never let a drunk person drive my chair again.

5. 2am is early evening now.

6. My bedroom light is nocturnal
   providing an evergreen-glow
   when it breathes in the dark.

7. Other people's sex
   sounds like an argument
   between a sofa and a wardrobe.

8. All the mirrors and quiet moments that told me that
   I couldn't do this were wrong.

An invisible war fought on three fronts

Lawrence Nicholas

I

I chew the gourmet toast my carer's carefully charred
in-time with my eyes' movements along to-do lists,

committing my morning of half-hour manoeuvres to memory,
hoping structure will keep diabetes in-check

and hold back the wolves prowling skirting boards,
searching my dressing gown for signs of weakness.

II

Fruit Pastels refill hollow veins
as Mirror Self bleeds across the windowsill,
taking aim at lightly spiced 2pm-pyjamas

"Every time you say, 'today's the day,' you commit to nothing
except failure. Look down. See those teeth tearing your toes apart?
If you had their motivation you might've reached the shower today."

A stolen piece of conversation,
snatched between reluctant-fire-door-groans,
breaks open hour-long silence; I cage my breath,

afraid flatmates will knock at any sign of life
and see the cost of an invisible war
fought on three fronts.

III

My first victory comes at eight o'clock,
when hunger reminds me how to use a light switch.

I take in the rubbles of my day:
every piece of to-do optimism strewn across the floor,

chairs full of clothes still locked in retail folds,
decide the best counterattack is my phoenix-wing thumbs

that forge wreckage into stanzas
and broadcast across cyberspace in poemcolour.

Someday

Lawrence Nicholas

after Frank O'Hara and Ocean Vuong

Someday I'll love Lawrence Nicholas
I tell myself, pretending
it's not a faraway dream.

The thing is, Lawrence,
those fiberglass clock-hands
are still there in your eyes,
trap-doorways to the night
you tried to become dust.

I can understand it, god, I've even
admired your strength sometimes
but that doesn't change the fact
you were ready to repay
every sacrifice your exhausted
evergreen parents made

by taking your own life.

Lawrence, I know you're still paying for it,
questioning every syllable said,
every cyberspace-sentence you send

because saying the wrong thing
means remaking the words you bled to the sky
after throwing that pillow aside.

Lawrence,
I know my armor today
is what you lived through.
I am here because you kept breathing
on the 90th day without sleep.

I can't remember what that felt like now.
I have Oxycodone-floorboards
keeping the monsters on leashes.

You had nothing but nakedness
against Great White Sciatic Wolves

surviving only
by counting teeth marks.

Lawrence, I'll never hate
you, but love
is a difficult thing.

Someday, the scars
will be smooth
and I'll file them away
like photographs.

Maybe then
we'll greet each other in a window
savour our morning coffee together
as friends.

Contacts

Summer Bramall: Instagram and Tik Tok: @sb.poe.try

Jamie Cavallo: Instagram: @jdcavallo

Imogen Cook: @birosmudged

Rachel Cunningham: rachellcunningham@yahoo.co.uk

Wendy Falla: pianolablues@hotmail.co.uk;
  blog: wendyslifelaundry.wordpress.com

Sophia Georghiou: sophiageorghiou@outlook.com;
  Twitter: @SophiaGeorghiou

Katt Grover: www.kattgrover.com; Instagram: @kattgrover

E.R Hollands: emmarosehollands@gmail.com;
  Twitter and Instagram: @ERHollands

Georgia Hilton: georgiahilton@me.com

Clare Holman-Hobbs: Twitter and Instagram: @_clobbs

Laura McKenzie: lauramckenziewriting@gmail.com

Henry Donald Marks: henrymarks@sky.com;
  Instagram: @HDM_beatnik

Gracie Marsh-Bawden: gracie_bawden@hotmail.co.uk

Stephen Mizen: ripper.live.events@gmail.com

Tom Moody: moodyt1988@gmail.com;
Twitter and Instagram: @tommoody_1988

Lawrence Nicholas: email: zignicholas@gmail.com;
lanpoet.com; Twitter: @LANicholas1

Molly Penney: mollypenney97@gmail.com

Beth Phillips: @bethanyphillips3@hotmail.com;
social media: @ragdollbeth

Mike Redman-Johnson: mikeredman@hotmail.co.uk

Mollie Russell: Twitter: @SpookySyntax

Olivia Sinthathurai: osinthathurai2@gmail.com;
Instagram: @Writing_Roses_500

Ellie Sparks: elisha122@hotmail.com;
Instagram: @justtryingtobeoriginal

Rebecca Ward: rebeccawardwriting@gmail.com;
rebeccawardwriting.wordpress.com

Antosh Wojcik: antoshwojcik.com